Dedicated to
my good friend
Asita and family
in Yogyakarta and to
my son Aden.

My First Book of
Indonesian Words

My First Book of
Indonesian Words

An ABC Rhyming Book of
Indonesian Language and Culture

by Linda Hibbs
Illustrated by Julia Laud

TUTTLE Publishing

Tokyo | Rutland, Vermont | Singapore

Introduction

My First Book of Indonesian Words introduces young children to Indonesian language (called Bahasa Indonesia) and culture through simple words that are part of everyday Indonesian life. Some of the words included in this book are specific to Indonesia while others have equivalents in languages all over the world.

Indonesian language is phonetic—it is spelled how it sounds. The vowel sounds (a, e, i, o, u) are usually softer than in English words.

Vowels

A – pronounced "ah"
E – pronounced "eh"
I – pronounced "ee"
O – pronounced "oh"
U – pronounced "oo"

Consonants

C – is pronounced "ch."
All other consonants are the same as in English.

Generally, in two-syllable words, emphasis is on the first syllable. In longer words, most emphasis is on the second-to-last syllable.

For example, in *"Apa kabar?"* ("How are you?") the emphasis falls on the first syllable of both words: A̲ pa ka̲ bar?
For words like *gamelan* the emphasis is as follows: ga me̲ lan.

Some of the words chosen have direct translations in English, such as *enak* (delicious) and *kucing* (cat), while others have specific cultural meaning, for example *batik* (wax drawn on cloth to make designs) and *dokar* (a two-wheeled horse-drawn cart).

Words that start with F, X, Q and Z are not found very often in Indonesian, but some English words starting with one of these letters have been adopted into the language, for example *futbal* (football or soccer).

Although hundreds of languages are spoken on the many islands that make up Indonesia, the existence of this shared language makes it possible for all Indonesians to communicate with one another. Indonesian is spoken by more than 240 million people around the world. We hope that this book will help that number grow by at least one. Happy reading!

A is for **"Apa kabar?"**
This means **"How are you?"**
I'm feeling well
and I hope you are too.

B is for **batik**.
Draw with wax, paint with dye.
When the wax is boiled off
hang the cloth up to dry.

A design is drawn onto cloth with
wax and then dipped in a dye
bath. The process is repeated.
When the wax is boiled off,
you have a colorful painting!

6

C is for **cicak**—
a **gecko** on the wall
calling "cicak-cicak!"
Careful, Cicak! Don't fall!

The letter "c" in Indonesian is
pronounced "ch."
Cicaks are very common in
Indonesian homes and make
a sound just like their name.

7

D is for **dokar**,
a fun way to go
when you want a ride
that's nice and slow.

In Indonesia these two-wheeled
horse-drawn carts jog along on
city streets. They don't go as fast as
cars but they can take you anywhere
you want to go.

8

E is for **enak**,
a word that means
Yum!
Like this mango
so sweet—
won't you please
try some?

Indonesia has a lot of sweet fruits like
mangoes, pineapples and rambutans, a
fruit that's hairy on the outside
but soft and sweet inside.

9

Futbal is a borrowed word from English "football," which in most countries is the game that's called soccer in the U.S.

F is for **futbal**.
That's **soccer**, you know.
I cheer for the home team.
GO, TEAM, GO!

Gamelan is a music ensemble mostly made up of gongs, drums and bronze instruments that you strike to get a sound.

G is for **gamelan**. Can you hear that sweet sound from the group of musicians who sit on the ground?

Most parts of Indonesia have a long
rainy season called the Monsoon season.

H is for **hujan**.
Rain cools the hot air.
Quick—find shelter!
There's water everywhere!

I is for **ikan**— **fish** swimming all around. A bright flash of gold swims up, dives down.

Ikan emas (gold fish) in Indonesia are big fish that are kept in large ponds. You can see flashes of gold as they rise to the surface and then dive under the water.

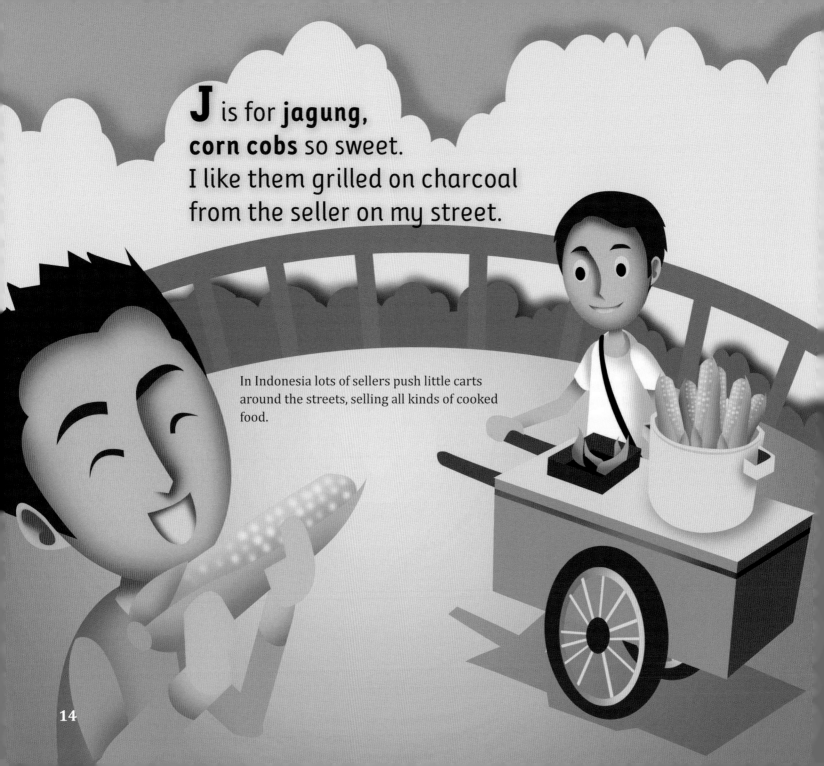

J is for **jagung,**
corn cobs so sweet.
I like them grilled on charcoal
from the seller on my street.

In Indonesia lots of sellers push little carts
around the streets, selling all kinds of cooked
food.

14

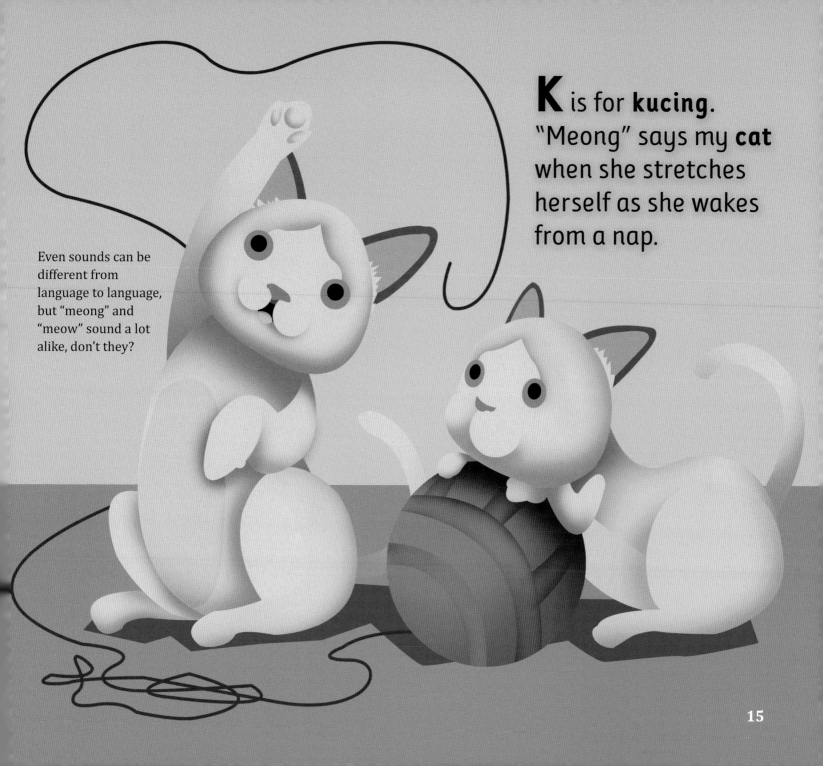

K is for **kucing**. "Meong" says my **cat** when she stretches herself as she wakes from a nap.

Even sounds can be different from language to language, but "meong" and "meow" sound a lot alike, don't they?

15

L is for **legong**,
a beautiful Balinese dance.
Two of us dance together
as if in a trance.

Legong is danced by
two young girls in
identical costumes.

16

To take a *mandi* you use a dipper to tip cold water over you from a tub in the bathroom.

M is for **mandi**.
Splish-splash—the water's cold!
"Don't forget to wash your face and hurry up !" we're told.

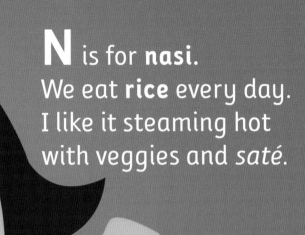

N is for **nasi**.
We eat **rice** every day.
I like it steaming hot
with veggies and *saté*.

Saté is marinated grilled meat
on skewers. Steamed rice is eaten
with most meals in Indonesia.

18

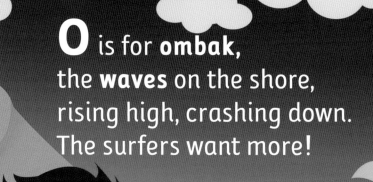

O is for **ombak**,
the **waves** on the shore,
rising high, crashing down.
The surfers want more!

The shores of Bali are a
favorite place for surfers,
who come from all over the
world to ride the waves.

19

P is for **pedas.**
It's so **spicy hot** you'll squeal—
Sambal made from chilies
we enjoy with every meal.

Sambal is a chili sauce that's very hot. It is added to all kinds of foods to make them extra tasty.

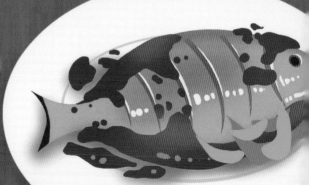

Q is for **queen**.
Ratu is what we say.
Look at her lovely gown.
Would you like
to be
Queen
for
a day?

Bahasa Indonesia
doesn't have words that
start with Q, V, X or Z.

21

R is for **rumah**.
My **house** is my home.
With my family all around me,
I never feel alone.

22

S is for **sekolah**.
Our **school** is lots of fun.
We learn and we have play time too,
to hop and skip and run.

23

T is for **terima kasih**.
"**Thank you,**" we like to say.
It is nice to be polite
and share a smile each day.

U is for **ular**.
A **snake** slides on the ground.
Tongue flicking to and fro,
he makes no sound.

25

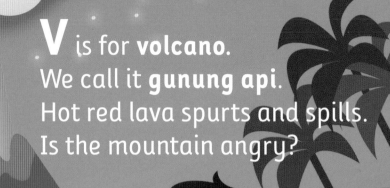

V is for **volcano**.
We call it **gunung api**.
Hot red lava spurts and spills.
Is the mountain angry?

There are lots of volcanoes
in Indonesia and many of
them are still active.

W is for **wayang**— a **shadow puppet** show tells fantastic stories of days of long ago.

Wayang are flat puppets made from leather. A light is shone on them and creates a shadow on the other side of a screen.

27

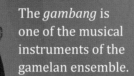

The *gambang* is one of the musical instruments of the gamelan ensemble.

X is for **xylophone**.
Gambang, we call it here.
It makes a mellow wooden sound.
Ahhh…can you hear?

When my mother asks me
"Do you want *ketan hitam*?"
I answer "**Y**a!" (that's "**Yes,** please!")
Coconut milk...mmm...yum!

Bubur ketan hitam is made from black sticky rice which is cooked to make a delicious sweet sticky porridge with palm sugar and a dash of coconut milk.

29

Z is for zoo.
Kebun binatang is what we say.
My friends and I wave good-bye.
"Sampai jumpa lagi"—let's meet again one day!

"Sampai jumpa lagi" means
"Until we meet again."

● LIST OF WORDS ●

"Apa kabar?" "How are you?"

batik a method of using wax and dye to make beautiful designs on cloth

Cicak gecko

dokar two-wheeled horse-drawn cart

enak! Yum!

futbal soccer

gambang xylophone

gamelan a music ensemble mostly made up of gongs, drums and bronze instruments.

gunung api volcano

hujan rain

ikan fish

jagung corn cobs

kebun binatang zoo

kucing cat

legong Balinese dance

mandi a traditional Indonesian bath

nasi rice

Ombak waves

pedas spicy hot

ratu queen

rumah house

Sekolah school

"Terima kasih" "Thank you"

Ular snake

Wayang shadow puppet

"Ya" "Yes"

Published by Tuttle Publishing, an imprint of
Periplus Editions (HK) Ltd.

www.tuttlepublishing.com

**Library of Congress Cataloging-in-Publication Data for this title
is in progress.**

ISBN 978-0-8048-5311-8
(Previously published under ISBN 978-0-8048-4557-1)

Distributed by

North America, Latin America & Europe
Tuttle Publishing, 364 Innovation Drive
North Clarendon, VT 05759-9436 U.S.A.
Tel: 1 (802) 773-8930; Fax: 1 (802) 773-6993
info@tuttlepublishing.com; www.tuttlepublishing.com

Japan
Tuttle Publishing, Yaekari Building, 3rd Floor,
5-4-12 Osaki, Shinagawa-ku, Tokyo 141 0032
Tel: (81) 3 5437-0171; Fax: (81) 3 5437-0755
sales@tuttle.co.jp; www.tuttle.co.jp

Asia Pacific
Berkeley Books Pte. Ltd., 3 Kallang Sector #04-01,
Singapore 349278
Tel: (65) 6741-2178; Fax: (65) 6741-2179
inquiries@periplus.com.sg; www.tuttlepublishing.com

The Tuttle Story
"Books to Span the East and West"

Our core mission at Tuttle Publishing is to create
books which bring people together one page at a time.
Tuttle was founded in 1832 in the small New England
town of Rutland, Vermont (USA). Our fundamental
values remain as strong today as they were then—to
publish best-in-class books informing the English-
speaking world about the countries and peoples of
Asia. The world has become a smaller place today
and Asia's economic, cultural and political influence
has expanded, yet the need for meaningful dialogue
and information about this diverse region has never
been greater. Since 1948, Tuttle has been a leader in
publishing books on the cultures, arts, cuisines, languages and literatures of Asia. Our authors and pho-
tographers have won numerous awards and Tuttle
has published thousands of books on subjects ranging
from martial arts to paper crafts. We welcome you to
explore the wealth of information available on Asia at
www.tuttlepublishing.com.

Indonesia
PT Java Books Indonesia, Kawasan Industri Pulogadung
Jl. Rawa Gelam IV No. 9, Jakarta 13930
Tel: (62) 21 4682-1088; Fax: (62) 21 461-0206
crm@periplus.co.id; www.periplus.com

24 23 22 21 20
10 9 8 7 6 5 4 3 2 1

Printed in Hong Kong   2003EP